CONTINENTS

Africa

Leila Merrell Foster

www.heinemann.co.uk/library

Visit our website to find out more information about Heinemann Library books.

To order:
☎ Phone 44 (0) 1865 888066
Send a fax to 44 (0) 1865 314091
Visit the Heinemann Bookshop at www.heinemann.co.uk/library to browse our
catalogue and order online.

First published in Great Britain by Heinemann Library, Halley Court, Jordan Hill, Oxford OX2 8EJ, part of Harcourt Education. Heinemann is a registered trademark of Harcourt Education Ltd.

Editorial: Kathy Peltan, Clare Lewis, and Katie Shepherd
Design: Joanna Hinton-Malivoire and Q2A Creative
Picture research: Erica Newbery
Production: Helen McCreath

Origination: Modern Age Repro House Ltd.
Printed and bound in China by South China Printing Co. Ltd.

10-digit ISBN 0-431-15812-6
13-digit ISBN 978-0-431-15812-9
10 09 08 07 06
10 9 8 7 6 5 4 3 2 1

British Library Cataloguing in Publication Data
Foster, Leila Merrell
Africa. – 2nd ed. – (Continents)
916
A full catalogue record for this book is available from the British Library.

Acknowledgements
The publishers would like to thank the following for permission to reproduce photographs: Getty/Robert Harding World Imagery/ Thorsten Milse p. **5**; Earth Scenes/Frank Krahmer, p. **7**; Tony Stone/Nicholas Parfitt, p.**9**; Tony Stone/Jeremy Walker, p.**11**; Bruce Coleman Inc./Brian Miller, p. **13**; Animals Animals/Bruce Davidson, p. **14**; Bruce Coleman, Inc./Nicholas DeVore III, p. **15**; Earth Scenes/Zig Leszczynski, p. **16**; Bruce Coleman, Inc./Lee Lyon, p. **17**; Corbis/Arthur Thevena, p. **19**; Bruce Coleman, Inc./Bob Burch, p. **21**; Corbis/K.M. Westermann, p. **22**; Corbis/AFP, p. **23**; Photo Edit/Paul Conklin, p. **24**; Bruce Coleman, Inc/John Shaw., p. **25**; Tony Stone/Sylrain Grandadam, p. **27**; Bruce Coleman, Inc./Norman Myers, p. **28**; Animals Animals/Leen Van der Silk, p. **29**.

Cover photograph of Africa, reproduced with permission of Science Photo Library/ Tom Van Sant, Geosphere Project/ Planetary Visions.

The publishers would like to thank Kathy Peltan, Keith Lye, and Nancy Harris for their assistance in the preparation of this book.

Every effort has been made to contact copyright holders of any material reproduced in this book. Any omissions will be rectified in subsequent printings if notice is given to the publishers.

The paper used to print this book comes from sustainable resources.

Some words are shown in bold, **like this**. You can find out what they mean by looking in the glossary.

Contents

Where is Africa?

A continent is a very large area of land. There are seven continents in the world. Africa is the second largest. The **Equator** crosses Africa. The Equator is an imaginary line around the centre of the Earth.

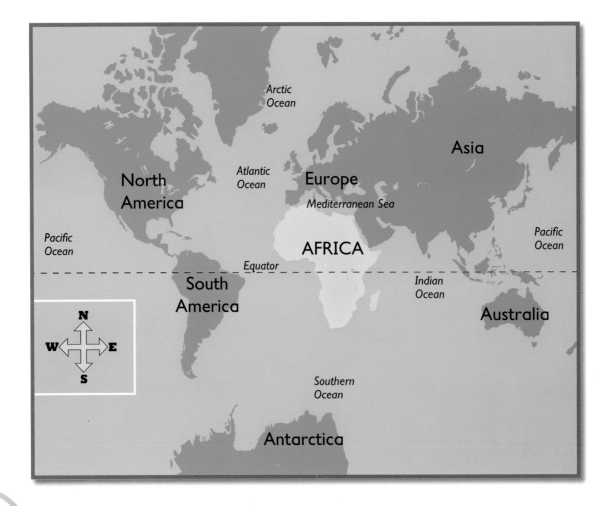

▲ *Cape of Good Hope, South Africa*

Africa lies between two great oceans. The Atlantic Ocean is to the west. The Indian Ocean is to the east. The Mediterranean Sea separates Africa from southern Europe.

Weather

Because Africa is on the **Equator**, it gets very hot. There are **rainforests** in Africa. The **climate** there is hot and rainy all year round. In some parts of Africa, the highest mountains are covered with snow and ice.

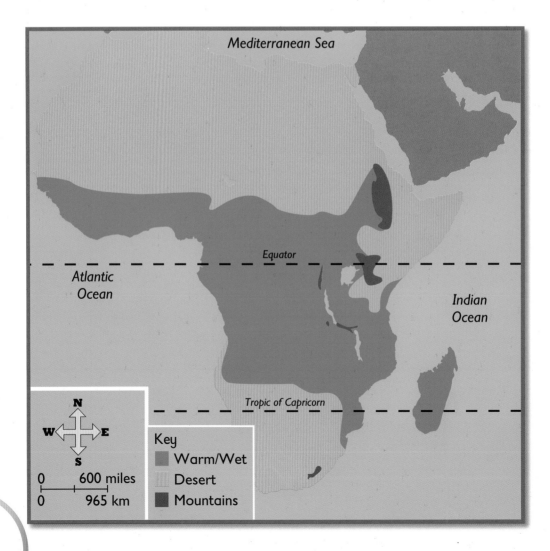

> The Namib Desert has the highest sand dunes in the world.

▲ *Namib Desert, southern Africa*

The **savannah** grasslands have a long dry **season** and a shorter wet season. It is hot all year in the huge **deserts**. At the southern tip of Africa, winter is warm and rainy. Summer is hot and dry.

Mountains and deserts

Large parts of central and southern Africa are high and flat. The mountains in East Africa include Mount Kilimanjaro. It was once an **active volcano**, but now it is **extinct**. This means it no longer erupts.

Mount Kilimanjaro is the tallest mountain in Africa.

▲ *Mount Kilimanjaro, East Africa*

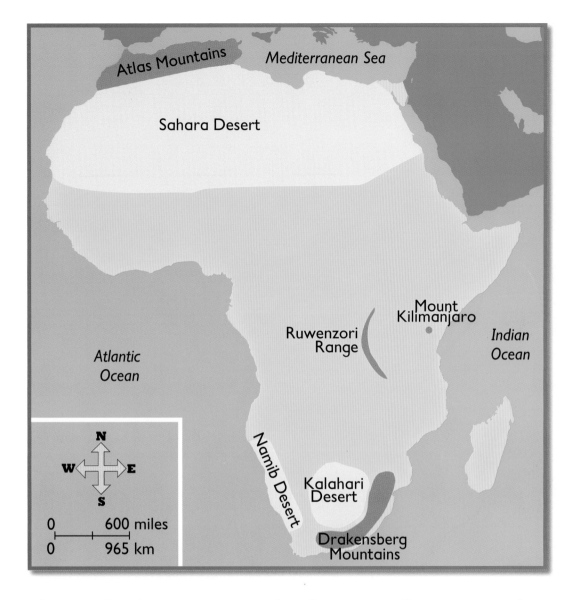

The Sahara Desert is the largest **desert** in the world. It covers nearly one third of Africa. In the south, the Kalahari and Namib Deserts are also huge. The hot African deserts have large sand dunes. They also have very hot winds.

Rivers

Africa has four of the world's greatest rivers. They are the Nile, the Congo, the Niger, and the Zambezi. The River Nile is the world's longest river. It has many **dams** to hold back water.

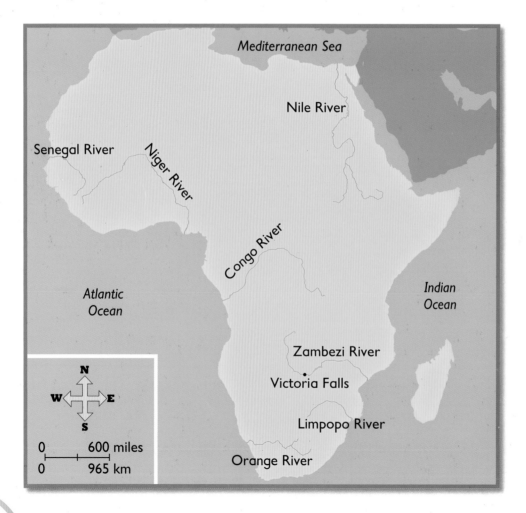

Mediterranean Sea

Nile River

Senegal River

Niger River

Congo River

Atlantic Ocean

Indian Ocean

Zambezi River

Victoria Falls

Limpopo River

Orange River

N
W   E
S

0   600 miles
0   965 km

The African name for Victoria Falls is *Mosi-oa-Tunya*. It means "the smoke that thunders".

▲ *Victoria Falls, Zimbabwe*

The River Zambezi falls 108 metres (355 feet) into a rocky **gorge**. This is Victoria Falls. People can sometimes hear the roaring water 40 kilometres (25 miles) away. The falls were named after Queen Victoria.

Lakes

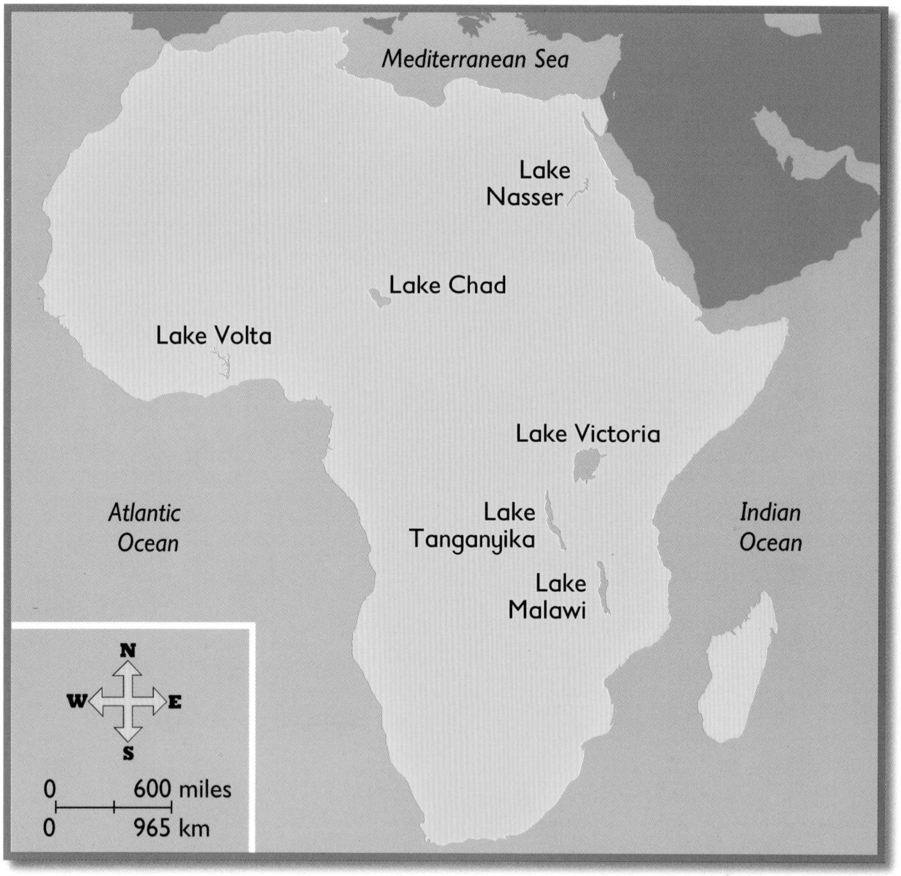
Mediterranean Sea
Lake Nasser
Lake Chad
Lake Volta
Lake Victoria
Atlantic Ocean
Lake Tanganyika
Indian Ocean
Lake Malawi
N
W
E
S
0 600 miles
0 965 km

Africa has many lakes. Some lakes were made when people built **dams** on the rivers. Lakes Tanganyika and Malawi are in the Great Rift Valley. Millions of years ago, land slipped down huge cracks in the earth and made this **valley**.

Many people live near Lake Victoria and fish in its waters. But now many fish are dying. Waste from factories and people has **polluted** the water.

Lake Victoria is one of the world's largest **freshwater** lakes.

▲ *Lake Victoria, Uganda*

Animals

Lions, elephants, and rhinoceroses all live on the grasslands known as **savannahs**. Zebras, wildebeest, and buffalo also live there. Giraffes eat leaves from the trees. Eagles and vultures fly in the sky.

▲ *Elephants in Kenya*

Many animals now live in **national parks**, where they are safe from hunters.

▲ *Gorilla in Rwanda*

Gorillas and chimpanzees swing through trees in the **rainforests** of central Africa. Crocodiles and hippos wallow in swamps. Flamingos and pelicans hunt for fish in rivers.

Plants

Thousands of plants and trees grow in the African **rainforests**. Some plants are very beautiful. Some are used to make medicines or food. People use the strong, hard wood from mahogany and ebony trees to make furniture and carvings.

▲ *Carvings made from ebony*

Thousands of years ago, the Ancient Egyptians used papyrus to make paper.

▲ *Papyrus reeds*

Papyrus **reeds** grow along the banks of the River Nile, in Egypt. Palm trees grow in many parts of Africa. Some palms grow dates and some grow coconuts. Sometimes people use palm tree leaves to make roofs for their houses.

Languages

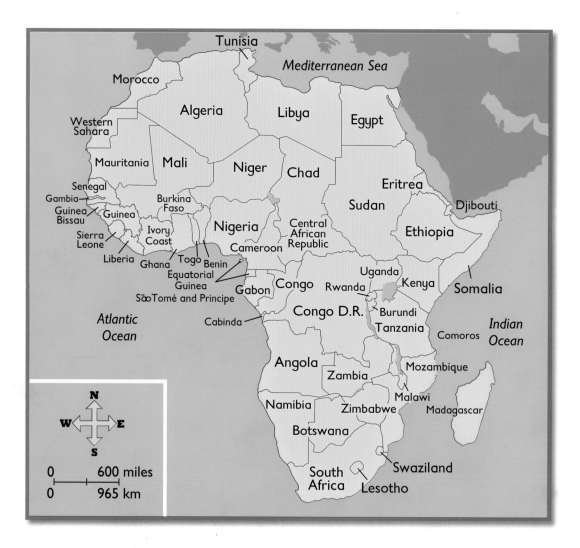

There are over 800 different languages in Africa. In the 19th century, many people from Europe came to live in Africa. Now some Africans speak English or French.

In North Africa, most people speak Arabic. This is because hundreds of years ago, Arabs from the Middle East moved to Africa. In southern Africa, most people speak one of the many Bantu languages.

▲ *Arab market in Egypt*

Cities

This map shows some of Africa's most important cities. Johannesburg is the largest city in South Africa. It was built by Dutch **settlers** in the 1880s after gold was discovered nearby. Gold is still **mined** there today.

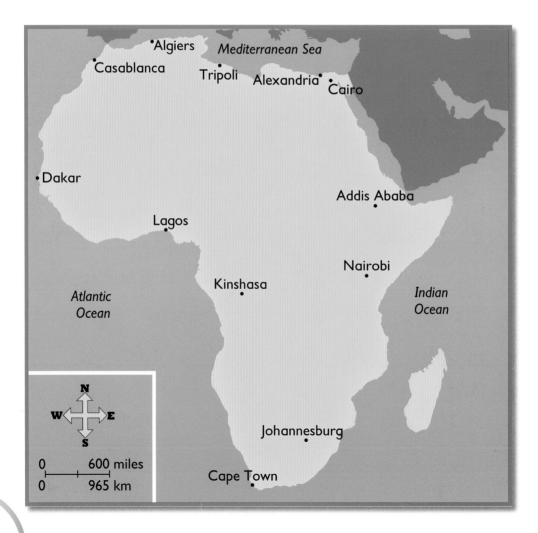

Cairo is the largest city in Africa. Six million people live there.

▲ *Cairo, Egypt*

Cairo is on the River Nile in North Africa. It is the **capital** of Egypt. Many tourists come to visit Cairo's museums. The museums contain amazing treasures found in the **tombs** of the Ancient Egyptians.

The roof of the Hassan II Mosque can slide open.

▲ *Casablanca, Morocco*

Casablanca is one of the busiest **ports** in Africa. It has many modern buildings. The Hassan II Mosque is one of the largest **mosques** in the world. It is on a platform over the Atlantic Ocean.

Lagos, in Nigeria, is a busy port on the Atlantic Ocean. Many people are so poor they do not have proper homes. They live in **shacks** made from pieces of wood, metal, or cardboard.

Lagos is the world's most crowded city.

▲ Lagos, Nigeria

In the country

Most people in Africa live in small villages. They grow their own food. Most villagers have farmed the same land for hundreds of years. In warm, wet areas of Africa, people grow bananas and **yams**. In the drier grasslands, many farmers grow wheat.

▲ A village in Guinea

Cattle **herders** keep moving to find new food and water for their animals.

▲ *Herding cattle*

Many Africans keep **herds** of cattle. The cattle produce milk. They are also sold for their meat. Some young Africans have now moved to the cities to look for jobs in shops or factories.

Famous places

The city of Timbuktu was an ancient **trading centre** near the River Niger. It had a large palace, beautiful **mosques** and a famous university. All the buildings were made of mud, so nothing is left of Timbuktu today.

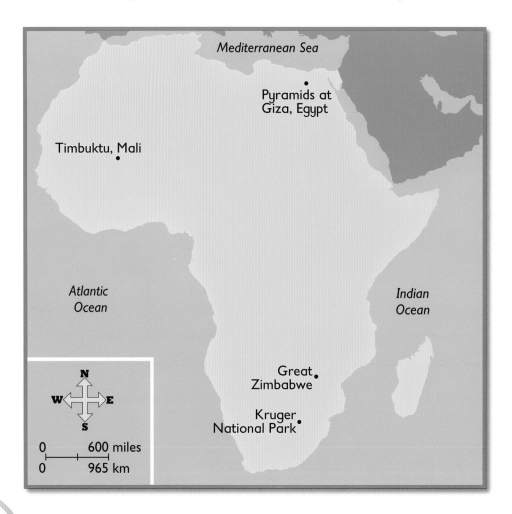

▼ *The pyramids at Giza, Egypt*

Thousands of years ago, the Ancient Egyptians built a group of stone pyramids close to the River Nile in Egypt. The Egyptians buried their rulers, known as pharaohs, deep inside these pyramids.

Only a few walls of this great city remain.

▲ *Great Zimbabwe, Zimbabwe*

About 1,000 years ago, people from all over southeast Africa began to bring gold to Great Zimbabwe. The rulers of Great Zimbabwe became rich and powerful. They built a huge city out of stone.

The Kruger **National Park** was set up in 1898 to protect animals from hunters. People go on safari there. They travel around the park to see the lions, elephants, giraffes, and zebras.

The Kruger National Park is the biggest wildlife park in the world.

▲ *Kruger National Park, South Africa*

Fast facts

Africa's highest mountains

Name of mountain	Height in metres	Height in feet	Country
Kilimanjaro	5,892	19,331	Tanzania
Mount Kenya	5,199	17,057	Kenya
Mawensi	5,149	16,893	Tanzania

Africa's longest rivers

Name of river	Length in kilometres	Length in miles	Where in Africa	Sea it flows into
Nile	6,695	4,160	North/East Africa	Mediterranean Sea
Congo	4,373	2,781	Central Africa	Atlantic Ocean
Niger	4,167	2,590	Africa	Gulf of Guinea

Africa's record breakers

Africa has more countries than any other continent.

The Sahara Desert is the largest **desert** in the world. It is almost as big as the USA.

Lake Victoria is one of the world's largest **freshwater** lakes. It covers an area about the same as Ireland.

The island of Madagascar, off the east coast of Africa, has some animals that are not found anywhere else in the world.

The Kruger National Park is the biggest park for wildlife in the world. It covers over 20,000 square kilometres (7,720 square miles).

The highest temperature ever recorded was in Libya, in Africa, in 1922. It was 58°C in the shade.

Glossary

active volcano hole in the earth from which hot, melted rock is thrown out

capital city where government leaders work

climate type of weather a place has

dam strong wall built across a river to hold back water

desert hot, dry place with very little rain

Equator imaginary circle around the exact middle of the earth

extinct no longer active

freshwater water that is not salty

gorge very deep valley with steep, rocky sides

herd big group of animals

herder someone who looks after a group of animals

mine to dig up things from under the earth's surface

mosque building used for worship by Muslims

national park area of wild land protected by the government

polluted poisoned or damaged by something harmful

port town or city with a harbour, where ships come and go

rainforest thick forest that has heavy rain all year round

reeds type of grass that grows near water

savannah grassy area with few trees, found in hot countries

season time of year

settlers people who come to live in a country

shack small, roughly built hut or house

tomb place where the dead are buried

trading centre place where many things are bought and sold

valley low area between hills and mountains

yam sweet potato

More books to read

My World of Geography: Deserts, Angela Royston
(Heinemann Library, 2004)

Watching Lions in Africa, Louise and Richard Spilsbury
(Heinemann Library, 2006)

We're from Kenya, Emma Lynch
(Heinemann Library, 2005)

Index